A Chill Wind Dawning

Published by 99% Press,
an imprint of Lasavia Publishing Ltd.
Auckland, New Zealand
www.lasaviapublishing.com

Copyright © Siobhan Rosenthal, 2020

This book is copyright. Apart from any fair dealing for the purpose of private study, research, criticism or reviews, as permitted under the Copyright Act, no part may be reproduced by any process without the permission of the publishers.

ISBN: 978-0-9951398-0-0

A Chill Wind Dawning

Siobhan Rosenthal

This book is dedicated to my sons
and comes with a million thanks to
a million wise, sustaining friends,
who will I hope forgive me for picking
one from the throng.
Special thanks to Julia,
who has been for so many years
a mother to me.

Thanks also to Creative New Zealand
for providing the funding, without which
this project would not have been
possible.

These poems and images were created at different points along the rocky road of recovery from a brain injury, inflicted by domestic violence. Naturally, healing from this kind of wound is a lifelong journey and the words and paintings shown here should be seen as steps along that path. Gifts sometimes arrive in unexpected ways: flowers blossom in the most unlikely and barren places. So it was with art and I, as I discovered in the wreckage of my former life and health a passion to draw, and a deeper desire to write.

These gave me hope during a dark period of post-concussive ill-health, when I was unable even to sit up on my own. When I recovered and left hospital, art and writing became the unexpected new bonds of a family that had to re-orientate around the unpalatable fact that I was too unwell to look after my own children. Without the backdrop of shared domestic life, our new relationship developed along lines of artistic communication. We discussed words and images endlessly, argued about whether computer games were art, and if poetry had any real point nowadays. They were kind enough to bring me examples of their own work, and gave me robust and honest feedback on my early attempts. If I have gradually improved, it is in no small part thanks to their earnest and serious encouragement.

This matters, because finding the confidence to be publicly creative is never easy. It's even less so when the body and mind have been pulverised by trauma and the road to recovery looks complex and uncertain. That this book came into existence at all is evidence of my sons' love, and a grateful testament to their critical encouragement and support. Without that, the courage to draw and write would certainly not exist.

"But other fell into good ground, and brought forth fruit, some an hundredfold."

A writing Class in New Zealand

We sit, softly pregnant with our futures, writing the past.

I saw a grass-snake once, back in the UK.

 An Australian home remembered falls apart the class,

As the writer sheds her critical skin, revealing tears.

A metaphor unpacked too deeply, like the snaking trees

Disliked by our tutor, because snakes are not of Aotearoa.

We protest our imagery's right to wander overseas

And defend the hellish landscape she identifies as unreal.

It would be better, novice students, to avoid such fantasies

Keep our writing sternly located and realistic, for now.

Outside the window, the vivid trees throw their leaves

In dramatic poses against the distant sky. Home was our topic

But it escapes me like the past, the distant cloud

The leaves that fall, unsettled, in a snakefree soil.

Body Surfing, Tahiti

He came towards me, tattooed like the wave

and his shark's tooth leant away, downwind,

the body board. I grinned, he swerved

And the moment crashed to pieces

In the foam, washed off

With the brown sand.

Forgetfulness is bliss, I know,

Yet tattooed the moment sways

a soul's shark tooth

necklacing me back

marbled memories a pearl

losing and finding the light

pricked forever upon my skin.

The wave plunges and returns

Yesterday's contentment

Is tomorrow's dream.

The rocks step away

into distant footsteps

ripples stitched

into the afternoon sea

quilt of time passing

dawdling pillow tide

a dark wave rises

along the shadow

drawn by the sun

I hesitate, then dive

swells close breaks inside

my protective harbour wall

gasp roll alight the wind

the world shreds

underneath him where

soft cream fronds dissolve

eases me to nothing

a promontory of love

Here the trickling sun

touches translucent leaves

breadfruit bends tree branches

buds hover like bees

slanting waves descend

rocks scatter up the beach

splendour reflected, noticed

a fruit returned to Eve

palm leaves bow like mercy

water mirrors sky

season of fruit and flower

garden of strange light

some purity of moment

a quality of sight

Pacific Birth begins

Red earth scratches my eyelids

and the dust road

jolts us across the island

a river of fire

burned out of the rock

a lava birth cord

tight around the neck

of an island so far gone

hanging off the world

precipice of life

a volcanic speck of dust

fallen out of the sea

clings to its edge

a tenuous mountain tree

white birds ride the currents overhead

look beyond

to a sky that no one knows

fall down

where the ground groaned and birthed

a canyon

No lagoon. The waves are closer here

yet when they crash down on the sand

it is a gentler tone, the music sounds in key.

Back home I heard planes take off, cannon fire

an ogre snoring drunk, sleeping off his frenzied rage.

But here they nuzzle the shore, calm, a child asleep

sucking slowly on the waiting breast.

On wilder nights, a muffled throb

the mother's heart rate heaves, holding tight

around the tiny island, pulse of life

unexpected growth spurt in the womb.

 I roll and wake. This sea swells

Gently vast, a stomach where

The baby kicks squishy hard

Against its sandy womb wall

Waiting to breathe land

And fizz onto the shore.

Pregnant she spun a wave

and birthed the fish

Ashore

She pushed me up like a mountain

shat me to the sky

vommed me up from Paradise

waited for my cry.

Don't take me yet. It's not birthtime,

earthworld above the waves,

let me nuzzle safe within

these underwater caves.

Hawaaiki, don't strand me here

on dried out sunburnt land

Pull me back inside you, from

their hot unfeeling hands

Give. And the rocks spread a little,

so the stones – flung by the storms ahead –

scattered wide enough

to push out the life

through the slit between two hills

a heaving pink canyon

gushes water

then sweat

joy birthed in its wake

slimy delight

cried patient

first breath

and he crawled to my nipple

contented

as though he and I

had all the time in the world

If you have killed a whale

now wear its tooth with pride

Do not fear the silence

of men walking by your side

If you have fished a pig

from the cliff down to the sea

do not mind the quivering

of those that did not see

When you have birthed a baby

when you have stretched and grown

let the world's waves part in awe

walk your seabed alone

Panmure Estuary

I held you in my arms.

The brash roundabout howled

louder than you, its songs as harsh

as the gale that blew February

out of the North Sea.

The creaking chairs that flew the sky.

Spinning specks of

                    light.

When you were older, I understood.

Scared of heights. You hadn't said.

Sorry, kid, I didn't know.

You changed, just like them:

Brexit, brex the experts, fixit

stop the boatloads blowing in

across the dank North Sea.

Old men sat in creaking chairs,

Spun sad specks of

> flight.

Today, that beach brings out its dead.

Deck chairs folded neatly, ended lives

ignored, abandoned, left to rot

like the ancient fairground

on a coastline that wept

with you into grey sky.

They die in creaking chairs

Spinning specks of

> light.

Here, Matariki dries winter days

into cold blue lightness, hemmed with kites.

Emigration flies strange routes,

But you're contented here, for now.

We evolved, to live. You stand your ground.

Still, the memory kite tugs upward.

Panmure Bridge. Drive steadily on.

Estuary winds a watery song:

back and forwards, town and hill.

The North Sea beach, a long lost haze.

There they die, and here we live.

The roundabout spins us in sky chairs

There's

death,

    light,

        relief

            for

                flight.

Howick

Yah, they built these nice new houses

Boxy-like but mint, sweet as

And then they only went and moved in this Housing NZ lot

No idea how to behave, noise, kids running around

Even the dogs let out to roam

No respect

And they're not even paying a proper rent I ask you

Oh, you're with Housing NZ too? Ah well, but

 you're, you know, a different type,

hey maybe you should ask them to let you move in

next to me, I wouldn't mind having you

living next door

Howick. The taxi stops

Throws me out

Before I can run away

back inland

Where I think I might belong

Toddler Dancing At Maraetai

Yeah nah, that day was alive like fire

Came by coach we did, straight up

All of us the whole kohanga,

Mums wear black skirts use your reo

Sit down listen good kids to the speech

marae time first then dance

kaumatua sizzling korero trickled joy

over us all like gentle rain

putting out a bushfire deep inside

in the ache of not speaking good

then flames up the Maraetai beach

sausages cooked by police

it was whakaute, man

respect and aroha like the tiriti says

my little boy he did his mihi

and we danced hundreds of us

Gangnam style hot sun

Now he's big and at Pakeha school

Daytime and I walk alone

Empty shell flickers on the sand

I hold it, memory, close

lighter than the breeze

there was a rahui back then

now you can collect kai again

black skirts dances skinny toddler arms

pick up those pipi shells when young

fish the wordkai out of the sea

learn the reo whilst you can

words fall light from wind, drift sand

Boy, you so quick to grow and forget

just a few words left shell-scattered

ash on the sand after the fire burnt out

There we danced and sang, you, me

Maraetai means meeting by the sea

Omana Beach

Omana beach. Cliffs fall to frills of sea

Wash-waka out in waves that leave the land

as awkward oars with staring eyes splash pee

tin cans and salt, towels, castle sand

detritus of the days when we could swim

before the sea lice came, that tearing sting

that lays instant rahui down, a grim

releasing of the sea to be, swear, sing

In its own sibilant speech; vast, alone.

Dark sun replies from elsewhere, spinning black

stormcloud webs, tendrils of turbulent foam

Her light spurts skyward from the waves - a crack -

and then it's dawn. The poem I want to make

is jettisoned. A swim I cannot take.

Paris: Sonnets of Divorce

I.

Because the Seine is just another stream

Because its bridges run like powdered tea

Unappetising, grey, a clouded theme

half-poured into a tasteless cup of me

Lost in this foreign city of my life

A tourist bored with travelling at all

half-ruined chapels, chateaux, bodies rife

with histories of pleasure and their fall

into the kind of wreck I am, that lies

one dredging operation out from home:

abroad, I sip instead this sludge of cries

from cats and men that wail the choice to roam.

Still, cityspires of patience bleakly soar

Endure this, body. Trudge it, door by door.

II.

My mother doesn't like me. That's a fact,
an inconvenient, unsettling one,
but undeniable, like death. That's that.
The memory of our friendship is cheap wine
of shallow vintage, bred on stony soil.
The fruit looked fine back then, until the time
I tried them out, believing in snake oil.
They crushed into sour grapes, embittered lime
that leaked into a pus-infested sore
The kind of wine you drink because you know
Sobriety is worse than sinking more.
Eventually I stopped. Less high than low
But that at least was when I learnt that shame
Matters less, alone. Now that's champagne.

III. Notre Dame

On fire night, the bloody nose that came

to everyone who loved her, and the île

from which she sprang that scarlet blossom flame

that mothered us in smoke, a smothered peal

of bells transmuted into sirens, rain

embraced by searchlights, bulging blackened walls:

hot sparks of history hosed down by the Seine.

I saw all that, initialled horror, awe -

Short-circuited impossibility -

The kind of shock that set it off, of course.

We wrapped our arms around the burning tree

and yet it crashed to ash. The shame. Divorce.

A building can be easier to love

than peace kept in a home. The burning dove.

IV.

Today is a bleak banlieue. Slabs of men -

grown tall like concrete cliffs - lounge, chasing ass.

Their butts are cigarettes, half-sucked and then

moon-dropped to smoulder out. They fart bleak gas.

Arrondissements of decadence and wealth

quarter themselves far off. A grand Versailles,

a gated world of gilt, sprawls somewhere else.

Its mirrors deflect luxury, half-sigh

at desperate women powdering their hair.

Outside, the shameless mud rides carriages

into the groaning ground. All life's unfair,

A heap of hungry corpses. Marriage is

not always a mistake: but it's a clue

if you agree, since nothing else will do.

V.

Where Tour Eiffel leaks light into the Seine

So falling metal ripples swirl in lines

 impressionistic dapples, gleaming vein

of many-cornered water, steel fork tines

that spear a shore engorged with greedy life.

Buy tickets if you want to try that climb

grind slowly up the spire: below, a knife

has sliced straight paths across the green. That time

you came when young, in love: to kiss at night,

of course. Bien sûr, the blushing, spooning game

of tongues and eating dew, joytrickling light.

The Field of War below was just a name.

Now mesh restrains you in the world you hate

along with those you kissed, and miss. So, wait.

VI. The Latin Quarter

Then, turning a corner, tapestry furled

soft rose-cupped gold, blushed on high-cheekboned walls.

Small-petalled stitches leafed gilt-captured world

A banquet of pastels, embroidered blonde curls

that flowed from a maiden brilliantly clear

clothed in virginity, silken, unreal

lost in the past, and yet strangely near.

She gazed, and I softened. Time seemed to kneel,

Impossible beauty, unicorn hair.

Remember her, sigh. Back then I could feel

that beauty brought joy and love worked out fair.

In Paris, time dawdles, blushing, to noon:

Clocks strike out innocence. Night falls too soon.

VII.

Eighteen, and Les Tuileries danced below

a carnival of wheeling light I soared

Ignoring the dark bridges, undertow

of life pulled from a river, scratched and clawed

the cats of Paris scowling at the nights

that shadow-closed the shutters, close to dawn

as waiters took the last carafe, and fights

began and ended in a sordid spawn

of men and fists. Quick women pushed their chairs

against the wall, kept back from flying glass

which didn't do much harm, those growling bears

thrown out into the wine-drenched chill. It passed -

and only young Tuileries roses seek

love in its wake. The red of my slapped cheek.

VIII.

In Paris, young, and a broken bed

that cupped us in as if we were the wine

our old hotel the glass, antique with dread

of what we filtered out, did not divine.

In daylight, saunters took us to Montmartre,

A white-tipped breast to savour in the north

Above a streetmaze, delicately dark

in which we slipped, loose-lipped, fell back and forth

as artists wrestle with their paint, and men

beginning revolution sign their names:

determinedly loyal. Blood ran again

from steak left bleu, the future bruises, shames.

I thought we'd stay behind those barricades

defend each other, love. Our picture fades.

IX.

Outside Versailles, she slaps me. Hard, as if

a teen girl could be forced down on the ground

and grow back, better-mannered. Hieroglyphs,

her fingers mark my thighs. Red shame rebounds

and stings when she reminds me, laughs. My tale.

I cope, of course, grow up and travel on.

Another era takes me in: I fail

to see the warning signs, get preyed upon.

I wonder if, that day, some tourists saw

Through power's gilted gates, sharp palace spikes -

That haughty queen, young serf chastised by law

and feudal rule, divine her right to strike.

After the revolution came more death

And yet I sympathise. That surge for breath.

X.

The Louvre? Why, it's a honeybee in flight

A diamond leaping skyward, thousand blooms

all fertilised at once as nectar light

drips insight, sweet as honeycomb at noon.

We stood in awe. "These sculptures have such grace."

He eyed them, also me, with shy desire.

"I really love the way they work in space."

The basement halls were dimly lit, a pyre

of other couples' passions, deathbed song

of who they were and wanted, long-damped fire.

Young marble limbs, entwined. Time, honeyed, gone.

Years passed. He saw the same, but love was dead.

"You know I hate it, sculpture." Enough said.

XI.

Yes, I remember that summer World Cup.

Brazilian drums, smart metro accueil.

The world crowding town, temperatures up

Some threat of strike. Parisians away.

I wish I'd stayed, to see the ball that hit

the back of the last net, Les Champs on fire.

But work moved me elsewhere. Leaving, I lit

a candle. Notre Dame, her pregnant spire.

Smoke flamed in dark. Above, rose window sighed

inflamed me, desperate for a better way.

A marriage, and three kids. The rising tide

Of miscarriage, abuse, ending the day

enough was too much, his hands on my son

too much else strangled. Whistle blew. I'm done.

XII.

Where it starts, the Seine looks like a mess.

It seeps through muddy ruins, Roman grime.

At the Orangerie my son saw depth

of colour, light, surprise. Artistic crime

committed by the young, who bore the rage

of broken rules. Impressionism born.

The Gare du Nord, a glass umbrella, shade -

Steel parasols and poems, now long gone.

Love sonnets, jerky, ruined. Shattered wife.

I got knocked to shit. Sculpture poorly carved.

And yet the children live to write their life.

The Seine departs from Paris, slugs into Le Havre.

Some boats command respect, just that they fight

against the tides of loss. That cloudy light.

Love song to my sons

I watched the sunset eat our world and knew

The times had fuck all left to say to me

It seems I possess nothing except you

Hot red, the sky sucked day out, dripped night dew

onto a grass-pricked graveyard, blasted tree.

It seems I possess nothing except you

Dusk sank into a frosty ravened hue

somewhere between despair and enmity.

It seems I possess nothing except you

At nightfall toothy hags sucked marrow through

this hollow stump of soil, skull-floating sea.

It seems I possess nothing except you

By midnight bony cobwebs seemed to chew

black holes that scattered moonlight potpourri.

It seems I possess nothing except you

However, I endured, I think: dawn blew

in bitter-tasting gusts, lifeboating me.

I watched the sunset eat our world and knew

It seems I possess nothing except you.

II.

So I, a torn love-letter, written through.

The flat-packed sign outside the superstore.

It seems I possess nothing except you.

Possession is the skin deep crime you knew

me guilty of. An idol of the law.

It seems I possess nothing except you.

The last ideal of melancholy, true

as stars are clear, and motherhood a flaw.

It seems I possess nothing except you.

It's wrong to keep another, but we do.

Words advertise my sin: poetic whore.

It seems I possess nothing except you.

A poem is first draft of history. New,

but written by the lost. A life-slammed door.

It seems I possess nothing except you.

I dance in empty air, discard the true.

Historians, like poets, kneel before.

So I, a torn love-letter, written through.

It seems I possess nothing except you.

III.

It burns like winter frost, birth, cuts you through.

The surgeon cloaked in green. His bloodstained boots.

It seems I possess nothing except you.

I watched it crack and mend, the scar you grew.

This belly belched and coiled, carved stretchmark routes.

It seems I possess nothing except you

A local anaesthetic. Slashed me to

the core of who I was, dark twisted roots.

It seems I possess nothing except you.

Three times they knifed me, forcepped you out, new

to me, this hollow world, life's raw recruits.

It seems I possess nothing except you.

Infected wound. Pus spurted milky dew.

Cracked, bitten skin. You suckled bitter fruits.

It seems I possess nothing except you.

Your midwives loved us warm, those tender few

who salved my stitched up body. Fragile shoots.

It burns like winter frost, birth, cuts you through.

It seems I possess nothing except you.

IV.

Unroll the past, consider, dream the view

a flying carpet pass-time, toy-specked floor.

It seems I possess nothing except you

and all you were and are. The times are new

and distant: now, a letter from before.

It seems I possess nothing except you

or where you came alive, a world in lieu

of being as I was, an empty shore.

It seems I possess nothing except you

my sons, my heart; the earth and sky withdrew

when you were made, or I forget before.

It seems I possess nothing except you

and what you gave me: memories I rue

for that we wept so little, so much more.

It seems I possess nothing except you

And then, and now: a broken rusty screw

I twisted back on childhood, lost. Ignore.

Unroll the past, consider, dream the view.

It seems I possess nothing except you.

V.

The end of needing love is death. Renew.

There is a loss in giving birth, of course.

It seems I possess nothing except you.

Renewal is despair, then getting through

To know what life both made and broke: remorse.

It seems I possess nothing except you.

A leaf that fell. A story to undo.

The nights without your suckling. Shame. Divorce.

It seems I possess nothing except you -

but nothing is a world of waiting, too.

I saw a child once tumble into gorse.

It seems I possess nothing except you.

His face was scratched like silver, and he knew

how childhood comes with scarring, too. And force.

It seems I possess nothing except you.

As elsewhere is a mystery, now and true

howls at the end, begins again, grows hoarse.

The end of needing love is death. Renew.

It seems I possess nothing except you.

Marae Time

I ought to die. The thought is clear.

I dream of turning in my life, it doesn't fit

These circumstances unbecoming to my mind

A refund is my right: or would be, were I just a soul

Not knitted out of air, and blood, and bone

Flesh that crunches frost, breathes smoke rings in cold air

I cannot want this body, life, but I can know this soil

The warmth that heats the cooking stones

The iwi wisdom, he tangata. People should stay alive.

Today the mountains scatter ash, hail agony, despair

Tomorrow, soon, a garden, rich volcanic earth.

It is the past I need to leave. This aching mind will heal

Accept its place in body, breath, the steady step of time.

The marae is a place of hope, patterned on the human frame.

Sestina On Sickness[1]

On those days, I juggle words into a tune

that plays a symphony of sympathetic paper

in my ears, smooth sheet music makes the bed

into a different sort of waking work, a road

where I catch syllaballs - attention - befriend

the juggernauting crowd, imagined extras in my film.

If Montaigne was right, we live on paper

in order that we may be better people, friends.

He disdained applause: or, at least, claimed the road

of self-improvement, as when he juggled duty, bed -

Then fled the plague, like some coward in a film.

But he lived on, to write. A grim survivor's tune.

---

[1] In Europe, medieval church authorities regularly preached against jugglers.

I remember him at times when my own road

is tumbling rough, juggling me; or I am back in bed,

Not miserable enough to die, just to need a friend:

more tossed about and flattened into paper

form, a scripted version of who I am: in tune

with those ideals I love and fail to live. This foreign film

I made at home - no crew - on location down the road

of solitude, sung solo, unaccompanied. A fancy tune,

I guess, though spun of endless sickness, bed

again. I lie, bored but lucky with my lot, that paper's

cheap: and nowadays juggling's not a sin: though bad poems defriend.

A thin world borders being, sleep and life. There poetry lays film

upon my eyelids, I paste it to another's sight - paper-

thin lenses, that's all I aspire to be. From bed

you scrape the world apart, see grit and tar, road

back to birth and death, all that. Montaigne lost many friends

to the plague he left. I'm dancing lonely tunes

juggling with my soul, condemning rushes of this film

I never meant to watch, can't switch off, unfilm.

Shooting daily takes of daylight, empty road

on which I scribble moments. Time a friend.

The poem grasps the nettle, as I don't. I paper

over my dark cracks, preach to silence, bed.

Life preaches on. I listen. Sheetless blankets scratch the record's tune.

Grains of Rice

Rice puddles are what life makes

when time is lost, turned into influenza.

All grey and pale, even breakfast

spooned from a tin. I should say, poured,

like rain which splutters fitful coughs outside.

The flu pools in my lungs. It spits me up. So be.

Thin phlegmy pudding puddled on my tongue.

Vague memories of kisses, dances, hugs.

Should there be drunken revelries, I'd sing

a song of social distance dropped like snow

upon a winter scene. So be. Grateful for flu, in part;

nothing worse for now. It sucks, but doesn't kill:

resembles me in general: subpar, but there.

Also tinned food, cold home, damp clothes

 and other inconvenient trifles.

I frippery my day with books and tea.

Television later, if I improve. All grey.

Flu curls around my throat and lungs

a sodden fog. Dull ache. I forget

if it is like this from flu, or flu is life

or something else entirely. So be.

You next, perhaps. The virus spreads itself

the same way depression, poverty, hope.

No one can tell what you'll pick up next. So be.

I wince for them out there, unlucky folk I met.

Can't say I didn't breathe, infectious life.

They sucked me in like sushi, bought

a week of fevered existential angst.

Rice shoots of sickness, growing fast.

Transplant to home. Pray them bed and warmth.

If I was tattooed, my bloody ink would say

"Sorry, I didn't know. Don't blame me."

No one ever thinks they are the problem.

But puddles are where the rice grows, too.

So be, and keep on being, just because

there isn't much to lose. Be life, if grey.

Cough until your chest is clear, or stopped.

Somewhere, a pair of coupling teens

shriek the world aloud with love.

Remember them. Life is. A storm, a veil.

Push it aside and kiss the world, despite.

Waterlogged, I cough: the teens' damp passion spurts

perhaps it's all the same, snot, mucus, sperm.

Life, a virus, replicates. So, be, and be again.

Rice paddies, rain. Like mood, mutates.

Eight billion grains. Here,

drizzle pots the straggled plants outside,

spatters rice puddles on malnourished ground.

Letter From My Soul

You're tired and hungry. The day is hard to love

given offhandedly by a disinterested world.

Dawn delivered with the newspaper, plastic-wrapped.

A free trial, but with nowhere to hand back.

The coffee stirs and pours you to awake.

What you need is not quite pity, but also not quite life

I think back then they used to call it hope: or death.

Not both at once: existence is the sprite

that dances out of sight, worthwhile in part

as long as you don't wonder why you're here.

There's half a film to watch. Enough to do.

Outside that fucker mowing, yet again.

You froth the milk, so life tastes right for now.

All of it is endurable, and yet.

In private moments, theologians will admit

The doctrine of the Fall is diligent but vague.

This is not a season for Edenic light.

You miss - all of it, I think, but especially youth

If you understood back then what you needed now

you might have balked. Hope is not

what will improve, but that we might endure

all of it plainly, without -

You kicked the ball, expecting life

to carry us to bliss. And now

the brokenness is not the figure or the rite.

More the grief you carry inwardly, respect

for what it isn't: simplicity of sight.

All that we see and were, and will become

is lost in paper, wished away like time

in the era where you thought breathing would improve

tomorrow might flow gentler if you endured

waited out the wind. So many fallen branches.

Still, you write.

What brick threw us through the blackened night

broke the barred window, to submit

with all our pain and indignation here

into this remote cell, towerblock of being?

What hideous love?

Flat Bush Buddhist Temple

I.

Ashes burn the dead alive again to flame.

Here dragons grow attentive, snarl awake

death fights my life puts it to sleep

throwing fiery tongues into the bitter air

above us with the flaming trees of light

Monks amble, chat. Clouds cluster,

orange sparks nudge awake the dawn.

Now chants hum broken flight drone wails

The statues pose bronzed metal sun

Hedged by grey wind

ants climb the curved walls

pillars later than sorrow flung

by machinery and thought

design implacable brick trees

Silent gong time

meditation on death is the highest form

unless you forget to live, when

 it becomes wrong death must not be sought

now ancient birds twitter beaks peck

 on the bare branches of existence

and annihilation clings to itself

a fruit left rotting on the plaintive tree

Death leaves me alone for now, it seems.

I am not light or shadow I am this

Limbs flesh and skin, blood witness eyes

skull hollowed out to take this mantra breath

If tomorrow comes it was not willed today

Just heartbeat breath continues

 yesterday's song again

bubbles break and form

stars burst to nothing drift on

this man's brother died alone

no feeding tube (dementia)

his words scrambled to nothing by hunger in the end.

They say it wasn't worth more life. Who knows.

Now I am not lonely or at peace

Hope has lost me in its darkness

Incense rises a sigh

best forget it now the funeral

we didn't manage to attend

going on

not home

clouds

alone

The dead do not speak.

Once written,

typed on a faded ribbon chattering the past

books in foreign language impossible to read

Standing steady on the shelf

Outside me look beyond

a courteous reader may arrive in time

Meanwhile I gloop the silence into paint

what's left of love splatters me with shape

so my dragons sleep peaceful on the page

somewhere else a raincloud

dusts the leaves with dripping light

Wild birds tame the slender desert temple tree

II.

The temple is all sky,

except where the land intervenes

The sea-red bricks honeycombed with stones

Somewhere else there may be bliss

but here today the heat

makes of life a sinking shroud

and breath a peripheral phrase

the spirit is fitful

even taste dies:

a fresh tomato

that I spoke

ate me dry

squeezed me to dust. I stood

dripped out in messy juice

squirted on the melting tarmac

a carpark of worshipping idlers

under the unfinished building

where builders scrambled scaffolds

in the hot bleak air.

 I wilt, and write.

Because they work

The temple is so new it shines.

Raw smoke trails blue and silver

into a livid orange haze

On the noble path within,

rock- hewn Buddha nods,

smiles alive a statue edged with trees.

Let each good deed

 last three thousand years.

I am waiting. Not sure for what.

This hurts like hunger,

shame, the rage for sleep.

Simply put, I am not yet here

as I could be, lotus-wise

instead a mass of jagged edges rip

my silences aloud. I burn the light.

Still, I try. We all do, now and again.

Looping thoughts curl into fringes

on the redgold lantern of prayer

incense drips ash from the waterfall of pain

Perhaps it is enough to know that

our feelings are the point of reference

whence bliss demands our loss

Whilst the gushing praise of life

Dribbles to nothing in the silent drought

of a desert storm

the whirlwind I saw swirl up outside

formed from dust in the road

a demon or a blessing tree

scattered ash on our lives

a woman bows down at the altar of loss

lights an incense stick

for no one, sorrow, people, me

And so we stumble forward

Each of us missing the point

as if the point is all there is

and missing it the story,

or the lotusgift. or the loss

Perhaps the end is silence

and this poem is all.

Perhaps there is a temple

higher than the cloud

Each flame attends its private song

in a recital given to itself, alone:

but still, companions come

to light the steady flame.

The incense crumbles black

Asks if I am really sure

of what I cannot believe

 If poetry is a missing link

Between the world and sea

where I stand, this cloister

impossible to see

what is built and what is grown

where you grow and where I end,

you and their ness:. he, she, me

Everything a passing breeze

all is seldom, never ends

except the sky holds up the tree

A monk explains they're closed.

I smile back, leave for now.

Tomorrow has a steadier look

of Buddha lost and found, despite.

A place where I shall sing the tree

and you will comfort, whisper

the leaves of you and me

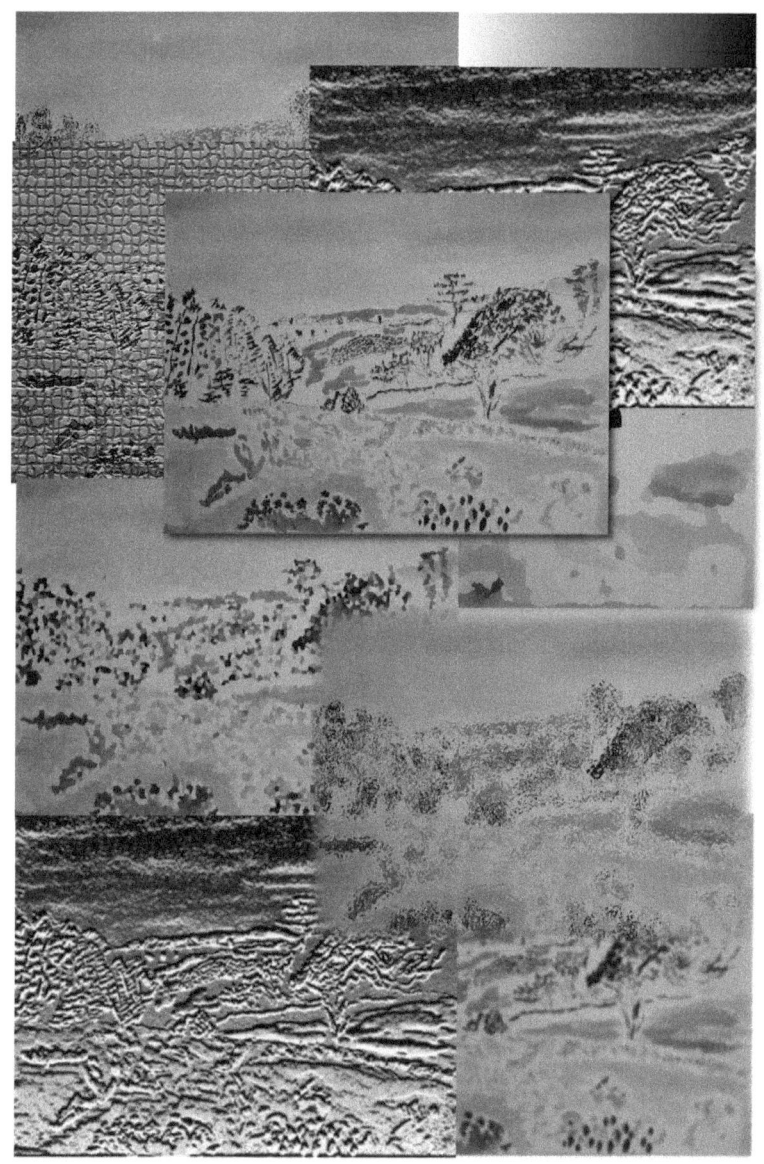

www.ingramcontent.com/pod-product-compliance
Lightning Source LLC
Chambersburg PA
CBHW061154010526
44118CB00027B/2974